SELF PORTRAIT
POEMS & ESSAYS

MAKENZIE CAMPBELL

central
avenue
2024

Published by Central Avenue Publishing, an imprint of Central Avenue Marketing Ltd.
www.centralavenuepublishing.com

SELF PORTRAIT: Poems and Essays

Trade Paperback: 978-1-77168-384-5
Epub: 978-1-77168-385-2

Published in Canada
Printed in United States of America

1. POETRY / General   2. POETRY / Women Authors

10 9 8 7 6 5 4 3 2 1

to grandma and papa:
i lost you both when i was ten years old
but your shadows are holding hands with me in my
twenties. your wisdom was lost on my young ears
but i remember all the things you told me
and i hold those words close.

and to a younger version of me:
you would be so proud of where we are now.

hi. i'm glad you're here. i'm honored you want to hold my humanity in your hands.

this book isn't one linear story. it's a handful of things i've experienced, in no particular order. i suppose we could blame that on my recently diagnosed adhd. it's always been difficult for me to piece big projects together into something cohesive. but maybe a coming-of-age collection shouldn't need to be. cohesive, that is. growing up sure isn't. my own coming-of-age sure hasn't been. the flow of these musings is a reflection of that.

if you've read my previous work, you'll know i write poetry. don't worry, there's plenty of that here. i can't help the poems that come. but i've also written of different parts of my life. of things i've learned. of things i've loved. things lost. things becoming.

it's a kaleidoscope of who i was, who i am, and who i'm shaping up to be.

this is the most honest piece of writing i've ever shared. my first collection, *2am thoughts*, was partially my truth and partially projection. that isn't to say any of it was dishonest. everything i wrote was very real to the human experience, just not always in conjunction with my personal experience . . . yet. i was seventeen, naive, and had barely scratched the surface of love or relationships or knowing who i was. i was a writer who daydreamed. my other two collections follow this style: i was writing from a distance, applying the things i saw and felt and imagined to some tentative version of me. the more i grow, the more i have in my life to write about, and the more willing i am to pull you closer.

with this collection, you're holding the skin and bones of who i am. you're seeing photos from my real life. you're hearing my inner monologue: my every feeling, the way i view the world at this age. you're up so close to my humanity i can almost feel your breath. and it's both a terror and a relief to be seen in this way. to allow myself the space to share in this way.

this is the beginning of my self-understanding. i suspect i'll spend the rest of my life uncovering and discovering and thinking i have it right—only to realize it's all wrong. and isn't that what we're all doing, all the time?

there's no magic age that makes us all-knowing. it's forever an unraveling of the self we are at any given moment. but how extraordinary is it that we're all trying to make sense of what it means to be human? i find a lot of comfort in knowing i'm not the only one lost.

and with that, i'm honored to be sharing this self-portrait with you. i can only hope you find pieces of your own reflection in these words.

this is my coming-of-age. thank you for giving it a soft place to rest.

contents

LOVE

ON LOVE

It's the thing we're all addicted to, isn't it? if we're not in love, we're dreaming of it, or we're cursing it, or we're questioning it. in some capacity, we're thinking of it. is this what the poets write about? yes. yes—a million times over. we can't get enough of this stuff.

i'm not only talking about romantic, whirlwind, fall-through-to-the-center-of-the-earth love; i'm talking about the friendships that fill our cup, the child who made us smile, the memory of the people who raised us. love takes many forms. it reaches all corners of humanity. it's reached out to me over and over.

i feel it ebbing and flowing through the earth, an energy that gives and takes but is never destroyed. love is the sun kissing my cheek. it's in the sharing of stories. it's in the time i flooded my 4x4 at one in the morning and my best friend held space for me to lay the weight of the world on her. love is in my roommate coming home from a weekend trip with a little gift because "this made me think of you." it's in the echo of laughter rattling the walls of a shared living room on franklin street. it's in the homemade birthday cakes my mom made me every year and the candles i'd blow out with the wish that we could all be like that forever, together under one roof. it's in the way i'm held by another person. it's in the sanctuary provided by their skin, the way it feels along my fingertips, and the way we stumble into six-hour conversations. it's the rabbit hole i trip into, the never-ending fall. i'm alice and i've made it to wonderland, and the wonderland is made real in the moment our eyes meet. in the comfortable silence we rest in. in the taste of sweet infiniteness it brings. it feels like the ground beneath me splitting open and tugging me as if to tell me a secret. the secret? no matter how hard i combat love, she will always force a surrender. her power is stronger than any will i have.

not that i haven't tried. not that i haven't not tried either. my relationship with love is ever-changing.

in my teenage years, i was desperate for it. always yearning. always afraid i'd never find it. but when i did, my fear shifted to worry i'd never find it again (so i'd better hold on for dear life to my first love). breaking into my twenties, i was in love with a man i thought i was going to marry. i was fully in the trenches, with tunnel vision. my fear of never finding love dwindled, but my addiction to it didn't.

now, in my midtwenties, i'm almost afraid of finding it again. it's a fluctuating balance between wanting someone to share my life with and feeling claustrophobic. i'm obsessed with the idea of my twenties being this chaotic, unapologetic, audacious era where i find myself. i'm scared a relationship with someone would stifle that. but do you ever really find yourself? and does keeping intimacy at arm's length lead to any real growth?

i'm not saying i avoid love at all costs. i'm a poet, for god's sake. even if i closed my eyes and locked myself in a room for the rest of my life, i'm sure love would find me. she always knows where i'm hiding. i fall in love all the time.

all. the. time.

the man reading a used copy of *the bell jar* at my favorite coffee shop.

the woman who took my hand in the bar bathroom and said, "i know we're going to be good friends."

the child who asked me to play stuffed animals with him on the sidewalk.

love is omnipresent, and this chapter is an ode to it. that longing. that insatiable want. and while i wish i could write about every person i've ever loved—that book would be much too long and way out of budget!—there are certain romantic loves that have profoundly shaped who i am, how i view love, how i feel it. although i swear, every time i fall again i banish the idea that the previous ones were love in the first place. when you're up so close to it, it's hard to see anything else for what it is. maybe because each love is dramatically different. maybe that's the beauty of it.

my first love was cherry red. it was fiery and naive and ill-advised and full of questions. and it touched the softest parts of me. it was the classic "girl falls in unrequited love with boy and holds it in the palms of her hands until it burns" affair. he was a boy who loved attention, and i loved to give it to him. he found his way into the majority of my first book. i don't have any words left for him, but i do have gratitude, for knowing how love can feel, for the lessons i learned. the moment i allowed myself to close that door was the moment i took a stance on my worth.

my second love was a deep blue. it was a blind dive with little insight into the depths or volatility of the water. i was happy treading until the first waves of hesitation rolled in over my head and i couldn't catch my breath. doubt was drowning the love i'd felt even as i feverishly tried to hold on to it. to grip the water. to find solace in his hands. but all i had were slick fingers. i kept asking myself, how did i get here? how did i lose the calm? i asked all the right questions a little too late. i came up gasping for air, and it surprised the both of us.

my third love was burnt orange, like a fleeting sunset. the kind you try to capture on camera but the photos never do it justice. something that can only be witnessed in full, in person. it ignited embers that turned to burn marks after he left. but not the kind you hide under long-sleeve jackets. the kind you wear proudly as if to say, "look! look at this proof that i'm alive and feeling everything. look at this bittersweet hurt that shows what it means to be human." it was a promise that love like that exists, in many hidden places. places i have yet to stumble upon. it took me a long time to let this love go—mostly because i felt robbed of an ending. the circumstances weren't kind. but after the tumultuous goodbye of my second love, this felt like a gentle hug. a reminder that love would return.

i don't know where love will find me next. i'm half convinced i'm in love as i write this. but i fall in love like it's an errand, and who knows how i'll feel tomorrow. what i do know is that she will find me again.

and she'll whisper,

"come here."

"come home."

i've been running from love for so long that i forgot
what it feels like to be held. i forgot how it splits your
heart down the center in a piercing war cry. how it
nurses you back to whole.
it's a conjuring.

every person we love

is another person

we can't untether ourselves from

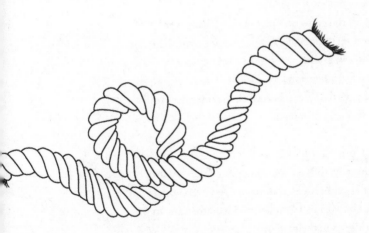

THE THING ABOUT FALLING IN LOVE IS

it's quick and clumsy and full of questions.

"so this is what the poets were talking about?"

it's exhaling your insecurities.
it's gifting them to gentle hands who keep them in
their breast pocket.
it's handwritten notes with penciled-in hearts
and texts that read "get home safe."
it's associating the word *home* with the shape of their
mouth.
tucking your smile into their collarbone when you
don't want to look too giddy.
because it's too early, isn't it? to be THIS in love?
it's three a.m. phone calls and fingertips grazing bare skin
when you can't fall asleep. it's the electromagnetic
force you feel when you look at them, i mean really
look at them. they are so beautiful. the most beautiful
human you've ever known.

falling in love is a trip to the center of the earth. it's the
way their name rolls on your tongue. it's the way their
shoulder tastes between your teeth. it's a deep hunger
to know every detail. to understand who they are. to sit
with your head in their lap while you ask them every
last question.

"what do you want to be when you grow up?"
"who was your first love?"
"what is the most beautiful thing about your mother?"

and what happens at the end of this?
is there an end to be worried about?
so many questions.
the answers are in the way they make you feel.
and for now,
that's enough.

"what did you want to tell me?"

what do i want to tell you...

i want to tell you that i haven't let last may leave my mind. i want to tell you it's been a twenty-four-hour cinema reeling with regret. i want to say that i've spent a lot of time alone. i'm very comfortable being alone. i want to tell you that when you said "i know you are comfortable being alone, but you don't have to be," a small part of me swelled. and a bigger part of me thought you must have ghostly vision to see through my walls like that. i want to tell you that i think i've been punishing myself for a long time. that i'm scared of hurting someone the way i hurt the last person who loved me. and so when you told me you told your mom about me, it all felt too tangible. even though i told my mom about you after our first date. i want to tell you i'm a hypocrite. that i'm full of paradoxes and i'm in a constant tug-of-war with myself. that i never once have known what i want. that i'm starting to think i might know but my voice shakes when i try to make decisions. i want to say that when you showed up at my party, all i could think about was how i wanted to hide away with you somewhere far from all these people. that you give me tunnel vision. that when our eyes meet i play pretend. cool, calm, collected. but my insides are melting. i want to tell you that when you look at me i turn to liquid. that i can't bear shape under the weight of your stare. i want to tell you that you woke something in me. something that's been in slumber for a long time. something i've kept caged. something that hasn't stopped, since may, clawing its way out.

i lied to my therapist.
which i know is the entire opposite purpose of
therapy.
but she asked me about you.
i told her i was scared of being in a relationship, not
because i'm scared to get hurt ("are you kidding me? i
would be *completely fine*"), but because i don't want to
hurt anyone the way i hurt him.

but looking at you now,
in this very moment,
i know you could break me in half
with the crack of a smile.

i'm not sure if i believe in love at first sight
but what happened between us
in those first few moments
was damn close
and i'm still trying to figure it out.
i'm not someone easily impressed and i'm not looking
for anything serious
and yet
that first conversation felt like a homecoming.
i never understood the danger of where this led
until you left
and then i fell straight down a rabbit hole of missing
and of dreaming of a future that nearly couldn't exist,
and yet i don't know how to stop replaying every
single thing you ever said
or the way your hands felt at that corner bar letting me
know i was wanted
or the way the world disappeared as you filled up my
whole vision.
you gave me the feeling of being alive
and i ran with it.
the city streets probably think feet
come in groups of four
because there wasn't a single road that didn't know the
rhythm of our steps.
we scaled that entire town without ever running out of
words.
if i got to keep you as long as i kept talking, i'd speak
forever, without breath i'd learn
because it's a deep hurt
to leave behind a *what if*
that could have been
if it weren't for the circumstances.

know i don't regret a single thing.
the most open and freeing feeling
was loving you even if it was brief.
with all the pain, with all the missing,
i'm honored you were a part of my story.

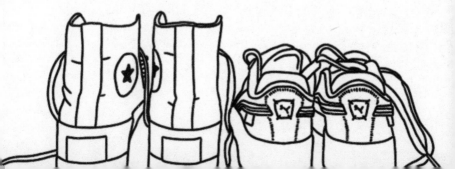

will you be patient when my walls won't come down
at the first kick
when my fears of commitment and making decisions
are at high tide
when i whisper i'm scared of this feeling
will you whisper back that it's alright to be?

it was soft and quiet and the most spectacular thing
i've ever experienced.
you opened doors and brought in light.
you found ways to unfold every detail of me.
and i shared with an open chest.
i wanted you to see me.
i wanted you to know me in my most intimate ways.
we weren't afraid of anything
in those moments, not even time.
we ran through the city and through the conversation
as if it would never catch up.
of course, it would.
but i'd swear under oath

that every time you kissed me you stopped it.

and when it finally did come knocking at our door, we
were fearless in that moment too.
it wasn't until after you left that i realized how much
i'll miss you.
i don't know if time or fate or whatever you believe in
will be kind to us.
i'm not waiting around to find out.
but if you'd ask me to come home,
just know i would.
i would.

IF I ONLY HAD ONE DAY OF THIS LIFE LEFT, HERE'S WHAT I WOULD TELL YOU:

that you remind me of a long lost friend / that on your lips i taste promises / the kind you hope for / the kind you keep / that when i look into your eyes i feel a deep belonging / that when you hold me i could unravel / and i wouldn't be scared / that you make me feel big / like i belong in a room / like i'm supposed to take up all the space / that you've shown me what falling feels like and for the first time in my life i didn't try to hang on to the cliff edge / that when i'm lying on my deathbed all i hope to see is our memories / our best moments / there are plenty

my favorite tree is the willow tree.

she is elegant and soft. her dancing is harmonious with the wind and she graciously gives us solace. a place to put our grievances privately behind her curtain. i can't tell you how many hours i've spent with my back to her dirt, arms strewn across her roots, letting the grief purge itself from me and sink beneath her soil. i can't tell you how many times she's borne the weight of your name when i could no longer. because the thing about the willow is, her curtain isn't just good for impromptu therapy sessions. it was for questioning eyes, a pair of hands in mine, a thought of "should we go there?" knowing we already had. it was stolen kisses and unbuttoning his jeans and whispers of the word *love* daringly. she watched as fingers circled my skin under her shade and how my eyes shifted when finding his, how two lovers were sheltered from the reality of what lay outside her branches. time stopped and i was foolish enough to forget that it would start again. but how beautiful to lose consciousness of who you are and how you're being perceived for the hunger to know another human being. this stranger that entered your mind like they already owned it. it was the only, singular thing i could track. his movements, his motives, the way his left eyebrow shot up at the cusp of a joke, his mouth on mine, on my inner thigh, how his smile softened my eyes because i'd never seen someone glow from the inside out the way he did. he told me he was afraid of endings. i wonder if he'd thought about ours. i wonder if he'd pictured it from the beginning, like i had. if he'd chosen to run through the wild with me anyway. finding the willow tree will always be the beginning of my favorite story. but stories have conclusions. eventually we had to pull the curtain back. and life didn't stop even when it felt like it had.

it just catches up to you. and then you're on a plane to wherever you came from before, despite being a different person now. because sharing something like that with someone doesn't not change you. you are forever marked with their memory and their kindness and their audacity to ever lead your linked hand underneath the edge of the earth, into that blip of time where nothing else exists. just me and him and the space we were so desperate to close between us.

do you know how fucking lucky we were?
people spend their whole goddamn lives looking for
what we happened upon. think how many pennies
tossed, stars wished upon, candles blown away. and it
came to us in the form of cosmic chance. a fleeting,
brief, singular aura of love shot between two paths.

now i wish for more time but we had what we had.
and i think about this poem every time your memory
brings sadness to my door. to think i found, at twenty-two,
what some people don't get in a lifetime.

and you hesitated on my front porch,
and the moonlight looks so pretty
spilling over your shoulders,
a spotlight
on this very moment.
i'm caught up in your almond eyes
and they're locked on mine
in a daring way.
it feels as if
i've transcended,
lifted by the flight
of this new feeling growing in my chest.

one of those moments where
you know the trajectory of your life just changed.

it's after our fifth date.
halfway through, when you were asking about my
family, crisscross applesauce on the couch, did i feel
the shift in me. if i hadn't known better, i'd think the
earth just split. i'm falling into her core.

on the way home, "enchanted" came on shuffle.
an ode to how you'd made me feel.
a lump started to crawl into my throat.
i'd had the most beautiful night and here i was crying.

it took me until the chorus to realize
the sadness didn't stem from you
but something deeper. something past.
a younger version of me used to cry herself to sleep
listening to this song and thinking about the
neighborhood boy whom she dearly loved, in a prayer
for him to love her back.

tonight, for the first time, i felt completely and daringly
wanted and seen. and that healed that younger version
of me who was deeply insecure and worried she wasn't
a person who could be loved like this.

you found me and took my hands and opened me up
as if to say,

"come here, come into the light, i want to know every
part of you."

A SONG I'LL NEVER FINISH (1)

the ghosts are digging up their graves
at the sound of your gentle name.
it's haunting faces in the dark,
it's memories leaving second marks.
they sit on my shoulder as if
their weight will force a listen,
covering my ears as they shout.
i've never heard the past echo this loud.
i'm tempted to let them take my hands
and ball them into fists,
raise them to your chest as if
i'm a sadomasochist.
i don't mean the bruises.
do you believe me?
it's just easier this way than admitting

that i've never felt so seen
and it fucking terrifies me.

you made me realize i've never been in love before.

the past claims names given to phantom stories.

"je te laisserai des mots."

i'll leave you these words, tucked between these lines,
as a tribute to the love i hold for you.
the feeling graciously sweeps over my body every time
i hear your name. five letters strung together and
suddenly it's poetry. i'll spend my life writing you
poems that only come half as close to the song your
mother gave you. but i'll adore you twice as much. and
offer promises i'll keep. because if i know anything, it's
that you are the most beautiful person i've ever
come to know and i'll spend forever marveling at the idea of
your hand in mine.

LOSS

ON LOSS

The hardest lesson i've yet had to learn in my twenties is how to let someone go. sometimes we are forced to by the people we love. they write us an ending and lock the door. we're left to clean up the mess. and sometimes we are the ones who bury the key. sometimes we write the endings. i wrote one without meaning to, without realizing it. and then i went back to dig it up, but i couldn't find where i'd buried the love i'd had. i remember feverishly searching. my shaky hands ran through our memories over and over. i convinced myself that if i just held them a minute longer, i could get back to that moment. i could feel as full as i used to feel. i begged and sobbed to all the gods to give me back my ignorance.

but that's the thing—once you have that thought, once you have that "maybe this isn't my person" punch to the gut, there is no going back. my mother has always told me i wear my emotions on my face, and this instance was no exception. i've never been a good actor.

and suddenly the boy i loved desperately for two years was slipping through my fingers. i didn't understand what was happening. i cried out in resistance, "i love him. i love him!" it was my winter song, the chant i clung to in the hopes it'd bring me back to my senses. he was kind and gentle and everything the younger version of me wanted. and here i was with him in the palm of one hand and the other reaching for more. for something else. reaching for whatever was in the opposite direction.

i think what scared me most was that it felt instantaneous. i went to bed with him in my arms, telling him how big my love was, and woke up to a stranger. but it was me who was unrecognizable. he was the same kind man. looking back now, i know there were signs. signs i refused to see. i was grasping onto what we once were so tightly that i'd tricked myself into believing it was still what i wanted. i ignored every message my body sent me, telling me to flee. and eventually the knowing couldn't be held back anymore. i was suffocating. the room we lay in was too confined. the world we built together was too small. i'd outgrown this relationship and i wasn't sure what to do. i held love for this man, but i was no longer in love with him.

i can't blame myself for being human. i was confused. i was scared. i loved a man i was going to say goodbye to. leaving and staying sat opposite each other on the teeter-totter, and i wasn't straightforward with him. i thought i could hold it together. i thought i needed some space to allow me to come back to his hands. but what i really needed was freedom. and by not realizing that sooner, i hurt both him and myself more than i intended.

before this moment, i'd known the heartache of others leaving. i'd known how it felt to hold unrequited love restlessly. i'd never once thought about what the other person might have felt. you can't be sad about a breakup if you're the one who caused it, right? but i was so inconsolably sad. i felt like my mind was betraying me. my mother picked me up at my university and for the entire five-hour drive home, i wept, and she wept with me. it hurt her to see her daughter that broken. i was a ghost of myself in that passenger seat.

my therapist put me on antidepressants for the first time. my friends tried their best to make me smile. some nights i'd let them drag me out in a desperate attempt at relief from myself—from the blame and guilt. other nights i wouldn't allow myself to leave. i'd skip out on plans only to lie in bed and ruminate on all the hurt caused by my hesitation. of course, i didn't yet know what was coming.

i didn't yet know that this had to happen. that there was more of the world to see than the small piece of it we'd shared. i didn't yet understand that as i grew and changed as a person, so did my wants and values and needs in a relationship. i felt stagnant, and the only way i knew how to break free was to let go of things that no longer served my growth. it was the hardest thing i've had to do. and it was the best thing i've done for me. because thinking about it now, i can't imagine being with that person. not because he isn't gentle and kind and lovely. but because i am a different person and i want different things, and i needed the world to touch me in this painful way to know that. there are people i have yet to meet who will feel like home. there are people who will challenge my growth. i needed this time alone to find myself and understand where i was headed. sometimes discovering yourself isn't something you can do alongside another person.

these next poems are placeholders for my emotions during our ending.

they are glimpses into what it felt like to hold on and how painful it was to let go.

i still hold love for him, and i still hold sorrow for the pain i caused. i hope he knows i didn't mean to. i hope he knows i'm sorry. i hope he's somewhere smiling.

i'm going
back to the
place we first
fell in love,
    but
this time
without the
lights on.

"I love you," he said.

Yet I still can't figure out how he could love me and leave me at the same time.

— as published in *2am thoughts* (2018)

it's here that i learned
that you can love someone
and choose to not be with them.
and it isn't cruel.
it's an act of self-love.
it's an act of honesty.

i'm not sure if my lovers would paint it in the same
light.
it's okay if they don't

because i didn't.

when i first had my heart broken he said he loved me.
i agonized over those words for weeks.
recited them in my sleep like a lovesick child.
wrote them over and over like an apology letter.
they were a concrete promise that i was loved
but not loved enough to stay
and i blamed myself for his leaving.

and for years i stuck to this notion
that love and leaving are antonyms
and one cannot exist in the same sentence as the other.
i even gave my friends advice on this.
to those i did, please know i was wrong.

because it wasn't until it happened to me
that i was able to understand what he meant.

"i love you and i'm leaving you," he said.

"i love you and i'm leaving you," i said.

and suddenly i became my own villain.

but am i evil for simultaneously loving someone for
who they are and realizing that doesn't fit with who i
am anymore?

realizing that fault is a defense that sometimes doesn't
exist. no one's to blame and no one's to say sorry. it
simply is what it is and the extent of my love won't
necessarily change that. i can love the sea and still find
myself drowning.

is it shameful to call it an act of bravery?
it felt courageous in the moment.
to give up everything i'd had
knowing it wasn't what i needed.
to perhaps not understand
but know
that what i wanted was no longer the same thing
and losing hours of sleep over the war between the
two.

we all know which one won out.

it's been a year now
and i still love them,
though in a friendlier manner,
and i'm still happy i left.
i stand by my decision.

i only hope one day, if not already, they can
understand.
i only hope one day, if not already, you can

understand
that you're not at fault for leaving or staying or loving
and leaving or being left and blaming.

that relationships are more complicated than they
seem and someone's leaving doesn't leave you as less.

THE THING ABOUT FALLING OUT OF LOVE IS

it's slow and arduous and full of questions.

"everything i ~~want~~ wanted (?) is right here, isn't it?"

it's a film reel playing back all your best moments.
it's a trick of the light.
it's melting ice in your hand and you're trying to catch it.
to hold its shape.
to will it back to its original form.
time has a funny way of making things unfit
themselves.
am i unfit for you?
other way around?
more questions...

falling out of love is growing pains.
it's realizing something's off, somewhere, somehow.
it's split ends you keep forgetting to make a hair
appointment for.
and it's written on the calendar.
and you keep picking up the phone to schedule
the appointment but you ~~forget to~~ don't actually call.
and why don't you call?
"because i don't know what i want."
because you don't know what you want.
but you do know you have split ends that
need tending to.
you do know you have loose ends to let free.
you know you have ends to make.
but how do you make them?
how do you say goodbye without a reason?

when it's a quiet, painful slipping away?
when there are still so many goddamn questions?

falling out of love is falling out of a piece of yourself.
falling out of love with a past version of you. people
don't talk about that enough. you fell out of love with
your partner. but you fell in love with them to begin
with. so somewhere between the falling in and the
slipping out, there lies a version of you you no longer
identify with. time has a funny way of making you
unfit for yourself. this is growth. this is growing pains.
this is the second goodbye you'll give.

falling out of love is a transformation. i hope you'll be
brave enough to move forward.

remember when i said i loved you
and it sounded like a question?
when i cried at the end of *500 days of summer*?
that's expected, right?
but what about the hour after?
was i supposed to cry then?
the extent of the characters
bleeding into our own love story.
their fate feeling familiar.

crying, again, on the way home from moscow
panhandle,
i wasn't homesick,
but in the absence of a reason
that's the one i gave you
and you held on to that like a promise.
the next morning i was homesick
and the following night
and you held on to those wilting words too.
anything sounds like a promise if you want it to bad
enough.

i can't apologize for being human
and not understanding
and for running away from warning signs
straight into your arms —
the arms they were warning me about.

but i can apologize for all the things i couldn't keep.
the promises, the scarf your mom knitted me, the
smile you fell in love with, that heart you so openly gave me.

i'm sorry for the pain i caused.

i remember calling up jordan with a sock in my mouth, trying fervently to ask her "have you ever had doubts?" but it all came out broken between sobs.

and i remember my mom being worried about me when i called her in the middle of january asking if she could pick me up from university.
"honey, the semester just started..."
and that only made me cry more. she came to get me the very next day.

and i remember the way she had her hand on my leg as i lay a lifeless form on the five-hour car ride home. she didn't understand.
"last week you were in love."

OBJECTS IN MIRROR ARE SADDER THAN THEY APPEAR.

and this week i'm in doubt.
and realization.
and all other terrible things.

i remember the static facetime calls where i'd talk to
him with my face in hiding because my mom always
said i wear my emotions there. i knew it'd be a tell.
how could i tell something i hadn't yet admitted to
myself?

i remember holding my heart and begging her to slow
down. begging my body to get out of bed. begging my
brain to fight this. it's paralyzing to know what you
need to do but never in a million lifetimes would you want to.

and i remember the cacophonic sound of a battered
ending. how the moment i said it i wanted to swallow
it all back. and i was sweating and crying as he asked,
"why? why?" — a film of guilt guiding itself over my skin.

i remember how the world was ending and i was the
one who ended it.

but i'm not sure what would be made of me if i didn't
do what i did.

(please know i fought it —
but if i won the battle, i'd still be the loser.)

I OPENED MY JAW WIDE
AND YOU CLIMBED INSIDE
AS IF IT WAS A GENTLE INVITATION.

AND I SWALLOWED YOU WHOLE.

i'm on a plane
but i'm going east instead of south
and it all feels wrong.
the seats feel smaller
and they gave me the goddamn pretzels i don't like
instead of the crackers they always gave me on my way
to you.

there's no "see you soon" message.
only the stale goodbye from three months ago.

my fingers hover
but when you're going east instead of south
you don't text.

if i was brave
i'd throw my buckle to the side
and rush to the cockpit,
pound my fists against the glass until it draws blood
and scream your name
over and over and over
until i felt the nose of the plane dive
and land in your city.

but i'm not brave
or bold
or fearless
despite all the times you said so.

i guess i'm not a lot of the things you thought i was.
i guess i'm not a lot of the things i thought i was either.

in the heat of heartbreak
i begged the gods to
let me let go of your hands
and now i don't remember
what it felt like to hold them
and i wish i did
and i wish i had
and i hope you read this and bring them home

i'm in the city.
 your city.
the one you always talked about.
i had a layover and missed my connecting flight
and now i'm staying in a hotel room that
alaska paid for somewhere near your neighborhood.
there are two beds in this room
even though i'm all alone.
it's like they know
i need a space for your ghost to rest.
the one that follows me to bed.
the one that climbs in my dreams just to remind me of
all the things i've missed.
i wonder how your dad's doing.
i know i never got to meet him
but you always said we'd make a trip to chicago
so we could eat your grandma's lemon meringue pie
and have your dad tell stories
of a younger version of you.
some days i wish we were younger
so we could have been friends
instead of this mess i made of us.
when you're five you don't know the pain
of growing out of a love you want to stay.
my therapist told me that
we worked in the past
and that's a tender, beautiful thing
but it's not something that works for me anymore
and i cried
because i knew she was right
no matter how much i didn't want her to be.
i ended therapy last week.
she said i was doing amazing.

she said i could handle anything life throws at me.
i bet she didn't think
life would throw me in the heart of your city
and beg me to call your name.
i'm sitting in this hotel room thinking
you might only be a few miles away,
which used to excite me
during all our long distance.
how ironic life is.
to take the distance away
only when i can no longer see you.
even though i can't see you,
i feel you in this city.
i feel the bones you built between buildings.
i feel the memories you had yet to tell me.
and it's both a comfort and a pain
to know i was loved by you
and to know i was the one who hurt you.

I REMAIN IN ALLEGIANCE WITH A PAST
VERSION OF YOU I'M FEVERISHLY WILLING
TO BE PRESENT.

you haunt the street corner
where you first asked to kiss me.

each time i pass it,
a flash of your memory's apparition.

i made you this ghost.
i turned this love cold.

so i know it isn't fair
to visit the grave i laid you in
with the same hands
that dug it up.

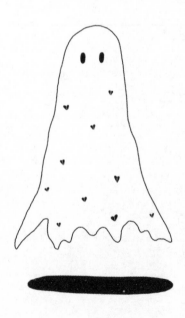

maybe this is me giving up
but it sure felt like i was in battle.

you act like i am the victor.
are there really any winners in war?

i stood with you for as long as i could
until my doubts swiped my knees
and you were left to write my eulogy.

i guess it's easier to make me the villain.
i can't say i wouldn't do the same.
i mean, how do you cope with losing someone that's
still an arm's reach away?
but not *your* arm's reach.
not *your* hand to hold.

for the first time in my life,
holding your heart in my hands
felt like a violent act.

i'm sorry my trigger finger hurt something so gentle.

the space between us is filled with empty peach pits

and promises to match

and hungry stomachs for a love that fills them more

than halfway

bloodshed on our memories.
it's so tiring
combating all these ghosts.

they rise from the past
like angry war vets,
a massacre mess
made by haunting shadows.

and i'll put up my fists
as if i can fight this,
but they've won before it commences.
it was all just for show.

MAYBE THESE HANDS WEREN'T MADE FOR
LOVING,

JUST LEAVING MARKS.

i thought i could tame you
into what i wanted you to be
but that's love on a leash

and really that's not love at all

when i think of october,
>   i think of the hollow of your name.
how it carved a soft spot inside of me.
how it made me concave into myself at every syllable.
how i fell to my knees when you asked me for
anything.

i still would if you were here.

they used to dress up on halloween to scare the dark
spirits away.

now i only dress up to hold hands with your ghost.

i've been mythologizing our past.
i needed to write that down to make it real.
is it possible to gaslight yourself?
i've dressed up my memories so much they hardly
resemble themselves.
i look back at the fires you set
and tell myself
how beautiful the sunset was that night,
pretending i didn't choke on the smoke.

you always believed in a god i couldn't commit to
but now i'm clasping my hands,
praying i can hold on to you,
wishing i'd gone to church so he would answer,
but your body has always been my sacred chapel.

PLEASE DON'T BE A STRANGER
after nicole ting

you've driven to my house so many times that your

apple maps recognizes it as "home."

i know it doesn't feel like it now.

i know the walls have lost their warmth.

but i hope you know they will never lose their

welcome.

i will always have open arms for you.

someone once told me that in the game of love,
it's either your head or your heart that's set aflame.

but what if
i accidentally set them both on fire with one match.
with one goodbye.
now all i'm filled with is guilt and smoke
and i can't find the clearing.
maybe there's no way to clear from such a crime scene.
there's yellow tape wrapped around
and they're trying to find a reason for the madness
but sometimes madness comes before the reasons.
sometimes love isn't linear.
it's all just a mess
of love letters,
and ash,
and dirty dishes,
and coffee for two,
and endings.
and i knew this but chose to chase it anyway.
it's human nature
to chase things they tell you you can't have.
or shouldn't have.
or should have but "not like this."
now i'm facing the wreckage
and while i wish i could say i regret it all
there's a comfort in knowing how it all feels on fire.
how electrifying it is
even if it demolished me.
even if it sent me to therapy.
and made me take pills for weeks.
a magnificent display of love and loss
and the war between what you feel and what you know,

and what you know is a goodbye is on the horizon.
what i can say is:
to know you
was a beautiful, tender, chaotic, painful thing.
but to not know you
to save myself from the inevitable fire
and "play it safe"
      would have been much more of a tragedy.

HOW FUCKING MAGICAL TO FALL IN LOVE?

HOW FUCKING EARTH-SHATTERING TO FALL OUT OF IT?

i'm learning how to let go of love.
it's such a rare, delicate thing, isn't it?
and so when it falls into my lap i do all that i can to
cage it in,
to claim it,
clip its wings so it only knows my hands as home.
but the truth is, often enough, love is a fleeting thing
or, perhaps, a permanent feeling for people who have
fleeting feet.
and they pass through your life on their own journey
and for one single moment you swapped stories and
shared a deep intimacy.
and called it love.
but love isn't always enough to change course
and so it lies there in your intersection
as something to mourn
but not something to take.
and i'm learning the beauty of love in passing
and love as experience
and how to let love just be.
because no matter how brief, how intense, or how sad
i become near the end of things,
it all proves that something beautiful transpired —
something gentle to hold — something to miss.

LONGING

Makenzie's
BUCKET LIS
❀ - ❀ - ❀ - ❀ -

☐ start a garden
☐ live in france for a year
☑ move away
☐ learn to give myself gr
☐ sing with a stranger
☑ backpack abroad
☑ write a book
☑ crash a wedd
   (respectfully)
☐ have every
   human exp
   to ever ex

ON LONGING

Leaving that man i loved for two years was the end of an era. i was starting from scratch. who was i outside the context of my relationship, my friends, my hobbies? i'd spent two months making a best friend of my bed, and now the sun was out and i wanted to feel what it was like to be happy again. i wanted her glow to touch my cheek and resurrect me. i remember that first day i felt a deep, radiating happiness after so many dark months—i woke at six in the morning while my roommates slept soundly. the birds were beckoning me, and i dug out my dusty ukulele to go sing with them. it seemed i was the only one awake in my college town, sitting crisscross applesauce next to the river, humming along with my vibrating strings, the cold of the morning biting my cheeks. it felt like a reminder that there were still good things. a reminder to come out and play. to allow myself to end my own crucifixion. this was my beginning.

and with this new beginning came the longing. for the things i'd missed. for the things i didn't yet know existed. for everything. i wanted to touch and feel and be a part of anything this world had to offer. i wanted to know the intimate parts of new people. i wanted to try new things. i wanted to disregard my meticulously calculated five-year plan in the hunt for what made me feel alive, which meant abandoning a lot of old parts of myself.

with this new longing came the fear. i no longer wanted simply to graduate, become a therapist, and get married. i also wanted to set off down the oregon coast and make a home in a van. i wanted to backpack the world with a one-way ticket and i wanted to go live in france. i wanted to try my hand at bartending and start a nonprofit with my sister. i also wanted to work more diligently on my writing career, but also maybe i wanted to become a lyricist, and then there's the piano i wanted to learn, the rollerblades i hadn't touched, so many strangers i wanted to know and the love i wanted to find in them. i wanted to experience everything, and i only had one singular lifetime to do it. what if it wasn't enough time? what if i didn't get to do all of these things? fear always asks the worst questions.

and yet those hard questions are the most necessary. they're the ones i most often return to. i've been gently rolling them over in my mind. ages twenty-one, twenty-two, twenty-three were all rich with this want. each dream was a helium balloon tied to my wrist. each new idea elevating me. the world was my oyster and i was on top of it—higher, higher, and higher. but at twenty-four i looked down and realized the ground was miles below me. i had no safe landing. i had no real attachment to anything concrete. in searching for it all, i had nothing.

the craving to not miss out developed into a fear of commitment. when you're deep in so much wanting, when you're faced with so many choices, the longing can immobilize you. it did for me. i couldn't commit to a career because there were so many jobs i wanted to try. i couldn't commit to a fourth book because i had too many ideas. i couldn't commit to a person, a person i felt a deep love for, because there were so many people in the world and what if i was missing out on someone else. a someone that didn't necessarily exist but could. they could! i'm beginning to understand that extending an arm to "what could be" instead of "what is" sometimes leaves you empty-handed and reaching.

but sometimes it offers so much you need both palms and more to hold it. so i guess we're back to square one. i guess you never know what you're going to get. that's what makes it all so risky. so enticing. but is there ever enough? when does the wanting start to sabotage you? at what point does it become sinister?

of course, i'm still brimming with desire despite my pondering the quality of it. knowing that something may be as bad for you as it is good doesn't stop the wanting. but recently i've been learning balance. i'm trying to teach myself how to dream for the future while appreciating the present. we can reach, but we have to make sure we also have something to hold on to. make sure what we're holding on to isn't a binding chain but a grounding anchor. make sure what we're reaching for isn't a glittering illusion but a beautiful truth that shows us its flaws—and that we want it, flaws and all. (emphasis on still learning.)

i've written a lot of poetry over the years to cope with all of this: the longing, the questions, the way they impact the life i'm living and choosing. some of these poems are about not knowing what i want. (do people ever truly know what they want? asking for a friend!) some of them are an ode to a longing i had for a person or an idea. some of them started with one intention and turned into something i'm not quite sure what to make of.

i'm not quite sure what to make of myself. i'm still so sick with want it scares me. but it also excites me, as i try to gently balance and honor it.

if we aren't longing for something, are we really living?

what does all this wanting mean?
i've shelved it for so long, i'm unsure.

after each sentence i have to lay down my pen and
rest.
it hurts to look at the tangible evidence of you.
the reconstruction of how you made me feel.
the bare bones of an almost love.
it was quiet and it was kind and i think that's what
makes it so hard to leave.
everything i want is in your hands
and yet, you have nothing to give.
i don't either.
the universe is cruel
for gifting us a long enough moment
to know that much,
but not long enough
to make something of it.

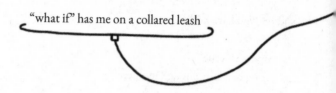

"what if" has me on a collared leash

what if i never find love? what if i do? which one is scarier?

what if i find it and lose it? what if i miss it in my fear to commit?

what if i'm not meant to love one person?

what if i like the soft skin of her stomach?

what if this is all just for show?

what if i've been pretending so long that i forgot how to be honest?

what if being perceived is scarier than living in shadow?

what if i'm never known?

what if the fear of being known so intimately will prevent me from letting people in? what if i never let me in?

what if i never understand myself?

what if i never reach my full potential?

what if i reach it, but keep moving the bar?

what if i succeed but never let myself feel it?

what if success is scarier than failure?

what if i'm so self-absorbed and anxious that i never allow myself to fail? what then?

what if my failures are all in my head?

what if time runs out?

what if i don't get to do all the things i said i would?

what if i didn't tell them all i love them?

what if the world ends?

what do i have to show for it?

what if there is no god?

what if we are all alone here on this floating rock?

what if death is just a quiet black hole we fall into?

what if she comes before i'm ready?

what if she comes when i am?

i know it was real.
you laid eyes on me and i unraveled.
that first night we sat on that worn, blue couch and let
our minds go wild. i blinked and seven hours went by.
a six a.m. bedtime never felt too soon.
i know it was real.
your eyes traced me walking into a room. i sat next to
you like it was reserved for me. i first heard you sing at
that karaoke bar where they played all the croatian
songs we pretended to know. you told me i was the
prettiest girl in the room. in any room. astounded
when i looked surprised, a troublesome crime i hadn't
come to this conclusion myself.
i know it was real.
wasn't it?
when our trains brought us back a month later to the
very same room. new borders, new language, but a
similar blue couch and that same curiosity. i told you
we could get coffee in the morning. tonight, i had a
date with an italian man and bottle of red. "text me if
he's boring." he was. i did. you picked me up on metro
six. this time you sang the beatles and everyone
cheered while you were beaming at me through the
crowd. beers in one hand, compliments in the other.
you'd thought about me nearly every day since. only
here will i confess, i did too.
i know it was real

because they said we argued like a married couple.
didn't they know we were near strangers? and yet i've
never floated through conversation so effortlessly. i
was falling towards the sky.
you were looking up, grounded.
i know it was real

because you kissed me in the hallway like you'd been
waiting for it for months. like that kiss was a
homecoming. it was singing in the streets and sneaking
into rooms. peeling clothes off in saunas and "i told
you so'". cobblestone roads and hooked ankles under
tables where our friends couldn't see. it was six hours
of aimlessly wandering the city because i didn't care
where i went as long as i had your company.
i know it was real
because you told me
...in another life. in a different time. in a world where
we weren't separated by ocean tides.
i know it was real
but sometimes i have to convince myself —
              opened messages with no reply,
              longing with loose ends,
              hopeless romantic meets a realist.

the realist knows when to say goodbye.
the romantic will spend the rest of her life
mythologizing it.

is it over if it never began?
i'll reach out with small talk,
some excuse to give you the opportunity to tell me
that letting this go was your biggest regret.

you've made your bed with other women.
i'm a single name strung on an endless list.
and it's alright, i have my own,
but yours will always have an asterisk next to it.
i'd set it aflame if you asked.

i've never known how to let things go.
you've always known endings.
well-versed in goodbyes
and not calling it what it is.
i thought you might.

"no one fell in love, right?"
i nodded,
complicit in my own murder.

every corner booth of a bar
reminds me of the way you
whispered my name.
hair tucked behind my ear,
the heat of your breath electrifying.
i might have blamed it on the alcohol then,
but i know what to call it now.

i wish i had been brave enough to call it what it was.

i miss the homes i've built in people.
the ones i can no longer visit.
the ones where i'd have to politely knock
instead of letting myself in.

the ones that wouldn't feel like home anymore.

NO SOLICITING !!!
we don't want your
services, cookies,
jesus speech, or
friendship.

as soon as the dust settles
i'll blow it all right back.
i can't seem to find closure
in the way i've forced our end.
it's like this that we'll be stuck
in our eternal loop.
i love everything
when it's shiny and new
so i dream up different plotlines,
new beginnings with your hands.
i'll promise this time will be different
and you'll believe me again
but somewhere in the middle
of our practiced dance
we'll get lost in translation,
fall into doubt and circle back
to the unfamiliar lovers
who don't know how to say goodbye.
so i'll say a "see you later"
and you'll nod, "until next time."

call this what you like, just not forever
because i don't know what i want.
there's evidence in the corners
of the old loves i still haunt.

a crash into new romance.
i wish i could be kinder.
i ignore all the yield signs,
i've always been a reckless driver.

you say you see me in your future.
you're planting seeds in rotten soil.
i didn't mean to make you bleed,
hit the brakes, flipped the car, recoiled.

i'll drive you to the hospital
they'll perform open heart surgery
but i won't be there when you wake.
it's a classic organ burglary

because you gave me your heart that first week
when i didn't ask
and i tried to be gentle
but i'm known to have unsteady hands,

ones that wander and are sick of want
and never know when it's enough.
will i ever learn
how to call my bluffs?

i'm a stick of dynamite,
always burn bright at the start,
but it is quick sparks and fleeting fumes

and you're left a stranger in the dark.

i hope you're doing alright.
i know i maimed you with my memory.
you don't have to believe me
but i meant everything

because i'm anything but a liar.
i just don't know how to close doors
and god i'm so tired of
trying to keep up with this greedy desire.
will i ever find what i'm looking for?

will i ever know what that is?

i'll slip between your fingers in the name of freedom.
but is belonging to nothing all that free?

i let go of an almost love
in the name of freedom,
but if i'm honest
it was really in the shadow of fear.

my mind made a bed for overthinking.
i run circles around the what ifs.
i'm so sick of tiring myself over minute things.
i'm so sick of flirting with the idea of things

but pulling back my hands when
they finally reach out to me.

i want to take back the time i closed the door.
i want to swallow back those words.
replace the space in my stomach
that's hungry for his hands.

i can make a lover out of you until you ask me to

you probably think i'm the girl that falls in love with everyone she meets. i've got a journal full of poems that coincide with that theory. but the truth is i'm a careful woman turned careless for an instant. i walked off that cliff without hesitation because it held the promise of your hands. and now i've fallen to the pit of it. that's what makes this so insurmountable.

SPOKEN WORD POEM NO. 1

i held on to your compliments like sacred promises.
when you're young you assume everyone's honest.

and when they tell you they love you,
they say it like they mean it.

but i love yous are transactions and, in my past,
the money never lasted.

but i believed in a dream and a boy.

i threw pennies down wells and wished for your hands
and when the gods didn't provide, i stole all my mom's
quarters and made more demands.

and eventually, my name found a way
between your teeth.
the way you held it sounded like a lullaby.
i'd spent hours under the hypnosis of that song.
only later did i recognize it as a war cry.

you told your mom you'd marry me.
a lover turned liar.
you told me you loved me last week.
it set my heart on fire.

and now you take it back?
it didn't exist?
holding on to your promises
with clenched fists,

praying
they won't slip.

but we all know they do.
we all know they have.
we all know the love you gave was never mine to keep
and the love i gave you was never mine to take back.

i'm so sick of love
and sick for it
a cycle i can't crawl out of

A SONG I'LL NEVER FINISH (2)

take your time,
it's alright,
i can wait.

i'll be patient
for the rest
of my days.

if you don't decide
by the time
i'm in my grave

tell them
to bury me
in your name.

the tide comes in and sweeps me out.
i thought it held the promise of solid ground,
but the sand sinks ankles the longer i try to stand
and the stability of your hands is nowhere to be seen.
lured me out on broken sails
and jumped in the lifeboat after the first violent wave,
and you drift away in peace
while i tear at the ropes to fight the storm you started and left me stranded in.
maybe you don't think much of it because you got away unscathed
but my ghost will occupy the sea.
so the next time you set sail in pursuit of another mermaid
my siren song of how you sunk me
will come haunt your ship,
and she may not hear it
but she'll see it in the way the color drains from your face.
you don't have to miss me
but you do have to live with the guilt.

you showed up like you were meant to be there,
and the life i knew before
got lost under the wanting.
everything i thought i'd figured out
shed its sense every time i looked at you.

WOMANHOOD

ON WOMANHOOD

I want to be able to tell you i've been empowered from the start. i want to be able to tell you that i've been a feminist all my life. i want to be able to tell you that i'm qualified to be writing an essay on womanhood because i've been fighting the good fight since i was a girl. the reality is, it took much too long for my eyes to become unclouded. and so, this isn't an essay on how the world has shrouded women, or the wrongs against women, or the strength of women. it's an essay on my becoming a woman. on where i came from. on how my desire to know and feel meant abandoning old ideas. on my journey of unlearning, and how that unlearning changed everything.

i met my first best friend in preschool. she had vibrant red hair and a voice that sounded like a lullaby. and, most importantly, a love for horses that rivaled my own. it was instant and we were inseparable. we shared apple slices at recess and swapped friendship bracelets and she taught me how to care for my tamagotchi. we binged *hannah montana* and sang along to the lady gaga music videos my mom wouldn't let me watch, and we gossiped about who the cutest fifth-grade boys were. and then middle school came.

in the seventh grade, she became sexually active. i didn't know much about sex then, but i did know it was something my parents didn't want me talking about. i knew it was dirty. i knew it was what all the boys made gross jokes about in the cafeteria. i knew girls' lunch conversations included anything but. so it took me by surprise, and i took it all wrong. i condemned her for it. i withdrew from our friendship quietly because i believed sex was wrong and icky and made you a bad person. it didn't occur to me until much later, into my adult life, that i never once faulted the boy. after all, he was just a boy. that's what boys did. it was our job as women to say no, right? it was our job as women to hold the boundaries, right? we were never supposed to want to have sex . . . right?

on my thirteenth birthday, my mom and dad took me out to dinner, just the three of us. this was strange because it would normally be the whole family (mom, dad, me, and my two younger sisters). but as the oldest, who rarely had alone time with her parents, i wasn't complaining. i was finally a teenager. that was big news! my mom placed a tiffany blue gift bag on the table. "it's for after dinner." i've never eaten so fast in my life. i was giddy with the idea of what it could be. a new phone? the coolest pair of miss me jeans? i impatiently waited for them to finish their meals, but once they did, the mood shifted. my mom became serious. my dad looked uncomfortable. i was unaware of what all this meant.

"this present is something that is very special to your dad and me," my mom said. "and to you. it's really important you understand how special this is."

i reached my hand into the bag and pulled out a little blue box with a cream-colored ribbon holding it together. i tugged the ends and it unraveled, revealing a silver ring set with four diamonds.

"it's a purity ring," my mom said.

i didn't know what that meant.

"you're a teenager now," she explained. "we need you to know how special your body is. we need you to know that your body is a sacred thing and shouldn't be shared with just anyone. we need you to know that some boys will want to share your body with you, but it's important you know that your body is only meant for one person."

my mom spoke while my dad continued to look uncomfortable, presumably because having the sex talk with his first daughter wasn't his favorite checkbox on the parenting agenda.

"you see the four diamonds? they all represent a promise. a promise that you will save your body for the person you marry. one diamond is for the promise to god. one diamond is for the promise to us, your parents. one is for the promise to him, your future husband. and this last one is for the promise to yourself.

"do you promise?"

"yes. i promise."

and that was my sex talk.

i took my parents' words as law, and i was an abiding citizen. for years, i held on to that ring like it would save me. from what, i'm not sure. what i am sure of is that i was the eldest daughter and nearly everything i did was meant to make my parents proud. if being abstinent would make them proud, i would damn sure do it.

you probably know where this is going. i think it's important to say that i don't hold any animosity towards my parents for this sex talk, or lack thereof. do i wish this conversation had gone differently? yes. but i don't see this as a reflection of their parenting skills, but rather the messaging they grew up with. i am incredibly lucky to have the parents i do, and i wholeheartedly believe they thought they were doing what was best for me. but i can't help but wonder now—if my parents had a son, would that talk have gone the same way? would he be receiving a purity ring and promising his body to his future spouse, parents, and a god he wasn't even sure he believed in?

and so i remained abstinent. i held judgment for people who casually dated in high school. i held even more judgment for people who were sexually active outside of a relationship. in my world, if you were dating, you were dating to marry. what would be the point of dating for fun?

i had my first real relationship when i was nineteen. you've already met him. and yes, i broke my promise. there was a lot of guilt and shame wrapped around my finger. i convinced myself it was okay because i was going to marry him.

the actual sex was … awkward. because i didn't really talk about sex with my friends, i didn't know what i was doing, or what i liked, or what i wanted. it wasn't until he suggested i try masturbating that the thought even crossed my mind—and the idea was met with immediate disgust. it took a while to unpack that. where did it come from? what was wrong with exploring my body? why were men allowed to talk openly about masturbating and the women i knew never once mentioned it? and why was i, only then at the age of twenty, realizing it? after ruminating on his suggestion for two weeks, becoming aware of the negative attitudes i subconsciously held and what they meant, i warmed up to the idea. it's almost embarrassing to admit my first time trying it was at the ripe old age of twenty. but i think it highlights just how ingrained these negative attitudes towards women's sexuality were. how impactful and heavy. i hope for other women's sake that my story is not typical. i hope it is the exception. but once i finally started talking about this with friends, i realized i'm not an outlier. the thought makes me ache for all the younger versions of us.

as i started to explore myself more, the sex with this boy got exponentially better, but the relationship didn't. as you know by now, he didn't turn out to be "the one." realizing this was gut-wrenching. after i painfully ended things with him and spent months taking little happy pills and not leaving my bed, i started doing these things i called self-dates. it was the first time in my life that i was being intentional about being alone and thinking introspectively. i would sit on a park bench at six in the morning, in that quiet hour before the rest of the world got loud and busy, and think about what i wanted. without other people's expectations, without other people's rules, without the need to be liked or the need for male attention, what did i want? who was i?

and in that line of questioning came my sexual awakening.

i'll spare my parents the suffering of having to read through their daughter's sexual history, but i think it's important to note that for the first time in my life, i felt like it was okay to want sex. it was okay to talk about sex. it was fun to talk about sex! for the first time in my life, i began accepting the idea that women were allowed to have sex with whoever they wanted, whenever they wanted, just like men did and were celebrated for. for the first time in my life, i wanted to celebrate sex for myself. and god, was it freeing to know i could make my own rules and i could raise a middle finger to the patriarchy who made me feel small and dirty for even thinking about it.

my sexual awakening was the catalyst to a much broader, longer awakening. i began to see things for what they truly were, not for how people tried to dress them. i now heard the misogyny laced through jokes and found i was not laughing. i stopped sugarcoating my anger to make men more comfortable. i'm still working on not saying sorry for the space i take up.

i started unpacking the societal rules i'd been taught that, for years, i'd mistaken for my own. i realized the only time i was shaving my legs was before i went on dates with men. that i wasn't doing it because it made me feel more beautiful, but because i knew soft legs were more palatable. so i stopped. i started questioning my sexuality. was i dating only men because i was genuinely attracted only to men, or because it was a deep-rooted lesson i'd learned as a kid? (boys liked girls and girls liked boys—that's it!) so i started exploring my sexuality. it took me three years from my very first thought of dating women to actively start seeking out opportunities and doing it. and—*big shocker*—i liked it!

somewhere amongst all these questions, the white sheet had been lifted from my eyes. i'd been complicit in a society that didn't benefit my gender. and with this realization came a deep anger, but also a deep relief. for when you know the rules of the game, you can start actually playing. and my god, was i ready to play by my own rules.

i'm still in the process of unlearning. of finding where antiquated ideas lurk in my subconscious. of untangling which values belong to me and which i've been tricked into adopting. of becoming better at identifying injustices and being brave enough to protect my peace even when it makes others uncomfortable. of the power of sharing and loving and growing with other women. i'm learning the strength of my own womanhood and womanhood as a whole. i was spoon-fed the patriarchy. it took a long time to realize i didn't like the taste. to realize there were other options, ones that left me feeling fuller.

when i told my mom how i'd purposely drifted from my childhood best friend because she was partaking in activities we didn't believe in, she was really proud of me.

when i diligently slipped that purity ring onto my finger and made four promises to save my body for marriage, she was really proud of me then too.

i'm sure she's not thrilled about reading all of this. dad either. but i hope she understands it for what it is—her little girl growing into a woman who is unapologetic in who she is. who's reclaiming her sexuality to define it for herself. who is writing about it because i think it's important for women to talk about. it's important for younger women to hear.

and i hope she is really proud of me.

there's an ache somewhere deep.
it's been growing ever since
i first learned what it means
to be conscious in my own skin.

THE THING ABOUT BEING A WOMAN IS

they tell you it's black and white / yet all they give is
greyscale / i'm always too much / i'm never enough /
my accomplishments are a tribute to how my father
raised me / my failures belong to my womanhood / if
i didn't have a father i'd be a poor, fragile thing / as if
being a woman on its own isn't power? / as if my skin
isn't strength / my presence a priority / conversations
about pay and appearance all beg the same question /
but they always have different answers / i'll let you in
on a little secret / the answers never benefit us.

when a man fails,
his failures belong to his
personhood.
not his manhood.

when a woman fails,
her failures belong to her
womanhood.
not her personhood.

so when we finally elect our first woman president,
i will throw up my hands in celebration,
i will be boastful with pride,
i will march through the streets cheering,
and i'll be sick to my stomach
because i know what's coming.
i know how they'll question and undermine her
in ways they would never dare a man.
how they'll debate her clothing
in relation to her intelligence
as if one has anything to do with the other.
how they'll blame her logical decisions
on her "hormones."
how they'll label her assertiveness as bitchy
but crucify her softer side as weak.
how they'll dig into her sexual history and use her past
as argument to why she's unfit for the position
despite the fact that a recent president
has been accused of sexual assault numerous times
and the people still vote for him.
i hope she's strong enough to endure
(i know she is).
i hope she's practiced her bark.
i hope she knows i'm always standing with her.
always rooting her on.

we had a moment under the stars where
we all got naked and slipped into
the warm water of the hot spring.
the milky way lighting up my cheeks
or maybe it was the childhood relief
of allowing our bodies to be bodies
and not something sexual.

our golden shoulders peeking out of the steam
and i thought how beautiful we looked in our skin.
how wonderful it feels to be open and free
in the midst of this canyon.
we could yell all our fears and dreams
and she would echo them
to whatever god is listening.

and we did.

     and we did.

being a sexual woman is so freeing.

i love my skin,

its softness.

i love the way my fingers feel gliding over it.

and over the skin of others.

the trace of curves and angles of the human body.

i love the sweetness of a new mouth.

the tender moments before they first touch.

the ravishment afterwards.

i love the freedom i have to say this now.

the freedom i've finally allowed myself.

i thought the end of the world
would sound like
hellfire explosions
but it was
the quiet distant rumble of a stomach.

i thought the end of the world
would sound like
hellfire explosions
but it was
the answer after *that* question.

i thought the end of the world
would sound like hellfire explosions
but it was
the soft sound of me choking on hard words.
it was the silence that hushed over stricken faces.
it was the police knocking on our door
while we wept in our living room.
it was the thrumming of our hearts sinking
for their friend, their family, their home.

there is so much anger between these walls
where there used to be innocence.
i wish i could paint over it
but there's no color stronger than pain.
she doesn't want to talk about it yet
and i respect her space.
but not before i tell her that it's okay.

> we don't have to talk.
> i can be an armrest for you.
> i can be a dam.
> i'll control the flood i feel
> and be strong for you.

even now, two years later,
we don't often explicitly discuss it.
but the burn mark is there.
a number of stifling, implicit embers survive time.
it's in the sound of our jaws locking
when a certain lana song comes on.
it's in the email thread between
her, me, and
an authority figure we no longer believe in.
for me, it's a secondary trauma.
though i will never come close
to knowing the magnitude of the pain
it's caused her.
writing about it allows me a shelf
to lay my anger down to rest,
though i think if i had the
entire world's supply of shelves,
it wouldn't nearly be enough to rid myself of it.
and so, the anger still exists.
at the person, at the system, at the greater society who
raise boys into men like this.

when will we stop teaching our girls that Blame is

synonymous with their womanhood?

when will we stop growing boys with greedy hands?

i hiked down the grand canyon earlier today
and the red sand left its mark on my skin.
someone told me to tell all my secrets to the earth
as a form of healing.
i've never believed in the god
my mother wants me to believe in,
but the colorado river and cicadas
are my form of a higher power,
and so i screamed into the desert
about how unfair the world is,
how i despise her rapist,
and the resentment i hold for the people who were
supposed to be the adults,
how i'm so sick of carrying this anger.
and the canyon echoed my rage.
i watched it all dissipate
to the bottom of the rock.

it's nice to have somewhere
to rest the heartache,

somewhere deeper than my gut.

i watch, retrospectively, my mother become a mother.
she recounts her twenties, only after i ask,
and i get to hear about all the hobbies
she used to have.
the parties, and best friends, and boys.
the art she used to create,
the mountains she used to ski.
(she hasn't picked up a paintbrush or pole
in twenty-four years.)
the longer she talks, the more animated she becomes.
her stories are saturated in desire.
maybe not to have these exact moments again,
but to have dreams again.
she grew up in a society that told her that
to enter motherhood was to abandon herself.
that the only way to be a good mother was
to give up who you were
in a devotion to the existence of your child.
and she did.
and i'm convinced she is the best mom
to have ever walked this earth.
but i wish someone would have told her,

"you can be the greatest mother and still prioritize
yourself."

the thing is
you can choose anything.

to shave your legs clean because it makes you feel beautiful
or to let your hair run wild,
to wear a pretty bra and hold them close
or to let your flesh hang free,
to save your body for one person
or no person
or a person you're emotionally connected to
or a person that you saw across the room that is so
undeniably attractive that it'd be a shame if you didn't.
just make sure you're choosing for yourself.
that it's *you* who is making the decisions.
god knows it took me much too long to start making my own.

crisscross applesauce in your bed
low voices and secrets without keys,
no need to tell you to keep quiet
about such a gentle thing.
you already knew how to hold it,
how to keep it contained
but not caged.
it's still sitting with you somewhere.
yours is holding hands with my shadow
and every once in a while
i feel your presence.
dutch braids and german cakes
baking during winter breaks.
i always thought our friendship was a lot like the way
your hair looked after i'd tied it,
one piece falling into the next until
there's no telling where one starts and one ends.
with you,
i always felt like we were existing in unison,
a transcendental being,
and time wasn't kind but it wasn't cruel either.
it just simply was,
and we just simply were
a tiny blip in this grand universe.

my women friendships have been
  the kindest i have ever known.

there is so much to be angry about, yes,
and there's so much grief to be had, yes,
but i would always choose this.
if i can't change it, i would still choose it
because i know the softness of girlhood,
because i know the echo of giggles,
i know the crisscross applesauce train
we'd all sit in to braid each other's hair,
i know the curves of their wrists as they place pink on
my face and the curl of our sacred pinky promises.
i know "dear diary" and swapping clothes and the
gentle space we hold for each other,
i know tiaras and dresses
and my mom always telling me
i was the most beautiful princess
and me believing her.
i know running into the lake naked without being
conscious of my body or what it looks like
or being wary of watchful eyes.
i know lying in each other's laps swapping secrets
while taylor swift sings through the speaker and the
trading of friendship bracelets.
i know the crisscross applesauce circle we'd all cry in
when our women came to air their grievances,
and though they belong to us,
they belong to us together.
we're a woven quilt with no real end,
just women among women among women,
and isn't it nice to know i have an army of them
who will hold my hand,
who will mirror my tears,
who will march into battle, should i ask.
it's comforting to know i have a place to rest it all.

TRAVEL

ON TRAVEL

I've marveled at the idea of travel since i was a young girl. i remember writing our bucket lists for a class project in the fifth grade, and i wrote a list of countries i wanted to visit: france, china, india, egypt. but this list was secondary. it was a surface desire. it was a "this would be cool to see if given the chance." this was before i knew what it meant to see the world. before i knew how small i am and how big the earth is. how full it can make you feel. how much it can make you yearn.

i took my first trip abroad when i was eighteen. i'd just graduated high school and i was cashing in the deal my parents had made me my freshman year. i was promised paris in exchange for a 4.0 gpa. we booked the flights before my second-semester senior year grades came in. (lucky me—i got a B in ms. holmstrom's calculus class.) and so a month after i threw my cap in the air, my parents and i were airborne on our first international flight, to london.

as i stepped off the plane, my whole body was thrumming with excitement. it was all so new. so inviting. i had everything planned out: nine a.m., see big ben. ten a.m., cross the london bridge. twelve p.m., lunch near buckingham palace. four p.m., camden market. this was tourism 101, filled with stereotypes and clichés. but everywhere we went, i went with wide eyes and wonder.

we caught a train to the heart of paris—my dream destination since i was twelve. this was my moment, and despite the groans and complaints you sometimes hear about this city, i was in love from the moment i stepped onto the platform. for me, the dirty streets added character. the art, a historical charm. we found a grassy spot under the eiffel and drank champagne and ate macarons, and i remember how the tower sparkled at midnight and my eyes welled with tears as i thought, i am here.

it left me wonderstruck.

this was what the world was like? this was what resided outside my small hometown? with that wonder came a deep need to see more.

i planned my second trip almost immediately after the first. where else could i go? what was available to broke college students like me? i found a cheap flight to germany, two friends who had no reason not to go, and booked it: three countries, four cities, fourteen days. it was my first time traveling with friends, and it was the first time i realized i could do it. we stayed in the cheapest places we could find, even if that meant sleeping on couches and riding rented bikes eight miles into town. this was tourism 201. we still made robust plans and we still saw all the touristy hotspots, but it felt more natural. we were more open to whatever opportunity the world might bring. a little more adventurous. a little more daring.

i planned another trip. greece with my two best friends. it was incredibly fun and incredibly not pg enough for this book. i'd graduated out of entry-level tourism classes and into a travel mindset where things weren't planned and guidebook checklists weren't made. this trip was a mechanical bull and we were holding on for dear life. bedtimes coincided with the sunrise after skinny-dipping in hotel pools and kissing pretty strangers on the beach. we met people from every corner of the earth and abandoned our plans so we could go dance at their house parties. we were drunk on the what-ifs of what could happen next, and i felt the world licking my fingertips with a kind of freedom i hadn't known existed.

i planned a fourth trip—big surprise! the world had been opened to me, or maybe i'd been opened to the world, and there was no closing that door again. i couldn't if i tried. i couldn't if i pushed all my weight against it. if i slammed a semi into it. there was no possible way to detach myself from what i now knew—that the world was so much bigger and so much more beautiful than i ever thought, than the movies could ever portray, than the poets could ever write about. that the only way to truly experience the world, and what it meant to be human, was to go. and nothing, absolutely nothing, could stop me.

i graduated university early and traded my last semester of college with friends for a single backpack and a one-way ticket. i realize i am incredibly privileged to have had these opportunities come to me and to be able to say my best friend from home dropped everything and came with me. and i'm immensely grateful to have these memories of parading through the castles in sintra, clubbing with strangers in madrid, taking mushrooms in the coffee shops of amsterdam, acquiring new scars in the streets of prague . . .

a month of this, and then she left. she needed to go home. i couldn't fathom the idea of it, so i stayed. solo. and while initially that terrified me, i've come to know it as the single best thing to ever happen to me. suddenly i had no plan. i had no one. i didn't know where i'd be sleeping the next night or what i should go see. and it was when i had nothing that i met the most interesting people. i had the ability to bend my trip into whatever shape i wanted. to bend myself into who i wanted to be, who i would be openly at home had i not been so concerned with trivial things and people-pleasing. and so when i met diego and he extended a free stay at his place in zurich, i went, and he introduced me to the city and all his local friends. and when i ran into a very attractive friend i'd met a month prior, i invited him out and let love find me on a new continent, even skipping my flight to spend one more bittersweet day together. the night he left, a stranger proposed i split a room with him on an eighteen-hour ferry to helsinki and i said yes. we got tattoos together the very next day and still facetime regularly, even though we only spent four days together in finland three years ago. but that's what happens when you travel. you risk it all. you break down your walls. you allow the strangers you meet to hold the most intimate parts of you because you never know when you will see them again. and isn't knowing you're on borrowed time enough to want to be known deeply by another person, even if only for a moment?

it was during this time that i was the best version of me. glowing with confidence, brimming with love. for the world. for the people. for the chance of being alive. i'd surrendered my expectations. in those moments, i didn't have to be doing a million things or working on my next book or finishing another master's course or chipping away at that iceberg of success that only grows the more i crack. my fear of time running out vanished because there was no choice but to be in the now. i was so busy seeing the world and finding new friends that i forgot about my finiteness. i forgot about futures and pasts. the only things that existed were my body, my joy, and the people i met that made me feel full.

i was free to be whoever i wanted. and in that, i became free of my obsession with controlling how i was perceived. i learned it's a hell of a lot easier to wear my inner self as outside clothing in a different city. and everyone, i mean everyone, loves the person who is unashamedly themselves. self-assurance and congruency slip on easily abroad, and they look really good on me. it's something to reflect on—why can't i bring that version of myself home with me? she's here, but she's only a fraction of herself. she's always half in hiding.

i've tried stuffing this version of me in my backpack. used all my strength to pull her onto that homebound plane. but she never seems to have a return ticket.

i'm not sure if this is a commentary on me or my home surroundings or perhaps the greater society i find myself both trying to dissolve into and be absolved from. there is a war somewhere deep inside my head, trying to separate it all, looking for a place to assign blame. i know i'll keep trying. trying to stitch together the girl who's uninterrupted outside her borders and the one who lives and loves within them. i'll spend my whole life trying. i can only hope with each return i'll be a bit closer.

until then, i'll buy another ticket to meet her. i can't wait to see her smile. to give her a hug.

to tell her i'm home.

the world opened itself up and swallowed me whole

and finally i understood what it meant to not be afraid

if there is one thing i've learned this far in life,
granted twenty-two isn't much compared to some,
but to me it's a whole lifetime,
i've learned how tender this world can be.
i've felt its softness across all my hard edges
and it's loosened me in a provocative way
because when you give the world your time and
curiosity,
it opens you.
it splits you down the center.
it nurses you back to youth.

i've been caged in uncomfortable situations
only to find the bars are set by my own limited view.
and i've been intrinsically frustrated by language
barriers and differing rules only to be reminded that
there isn't one of anything normative.
that we're all human, trying to make it.
trying to find our way.
and once that door was open to an alternative
i found a world of opportunity for growth and learning
and learning to lead a life with love.

i've been split and i'm finding i only feel more full.

the more i surrender myself to the idea that home isn't
a place but a feeling hidden within every place i go,
the more intimately i let the world touch me and the
more intensely i feel her calling out my name.

we are all in mourning for the lives we didn't get to

live

as consequence to the one we chose

in a little red chair
with a packed lunch for school
i learned that sixty seconds fold into a minute
and sixty minutes are traded for an hour
and the concept of time was told
like a nonfiction storybook
where it all made sense and felt real and tangible.
and now, sitting here, on this little blue chair
with a packed lunch for the train ride
out of a city i've spent three days in
and have the urge to now call home,
i'm learning that
time is as elusive as the northern lights,
minutes can feel like hours
in the right company,
mere hours can feel like decades
in the right city,
the concept of time is no longer my storybook
but now my memoir.
three days spent with a stranger
and i know more about them than i know about
lifelong friends back home.
people will say days aren't enough to create viable
friendships or fall in love,
but when you're up this close with time,
when you're staring in its selfish eyes,
knowing you have so little,
you play the game as if you have nothing to lose
and you spill the intimate parts of yourself
almost desperately into others
in a way to make up for what's lost and will soon be,
and though you can never defeat her,
this is your act of defiance

and in this act
time fades into oblivion.
there's just you and these strangers
and this very moment,
alive and beautiful and smiling.

i'm so much bigger than i
thought i was!

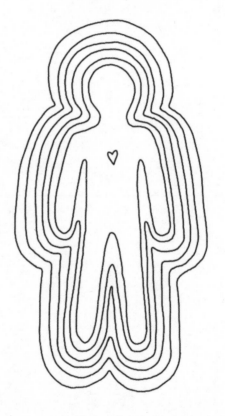

i'm so much smaller than i
thought i was.

and when i think of that city
i think of your name
and how it's tethered there.
one cannot exist without the other.
i cannot relive those moments without you in mind.
we scoured every inch of that town
for the sake of wanderlust,
and each moment will be tucked away
as a sacred memory
of what it means to travel,
of what it means to be open.
yesterday you were a stranger
but now i know your heart as if it is my own.
a chance encounter,
a brief blip in time.
but the stories i'll tell,
yours will always be intertwined.

i hope when your little boy asks
about the first girl you loved,
i hope you tell him my name.
i hope when your mom asks how your travels were
you'll have a sheepish smile
at my memory.
i hope you never think me a stranger
because i know no matter how hard i could try
i would never be able to unknow you.
i wouldn't want to.
all the hours running through the dim lit city streets,
conversations where i'd never felt more seen.
the locals in that town still murmur our story
and yet
a false forever with a whiplash ending.
we came and passed each other so quickly.
i wish i could freeze-frame every time you kissed me
but you can't stop the hands of time
and we can't pause on a what could have been.
but just know
out of every what if,
you are my favorite.

maastricht

berne

stockholm

i'm on the second stair of my back porch
of my little house on this quiet night
listening to "ribs" and looking up
at the stars.
you can't really see them in the heart of denver
but i know they're there.
it reminds me of how small i am.
it reminds me, too,
how far my heart has been spread.
there are pieces of me
in holland and peru and stockholm
carried by the hands of strangers
i came to know as home
for a passing moment.
a soft smile echoes to the sky.
i'm happy to share this little life
with them all.
i'm happy to know how vast this world is,
and to know love reaches every last corner.

that love found me in the most unexpected of places.

there are so many beautiful people in this world
and i'm mourning the fact that i won't get to meet
most of them

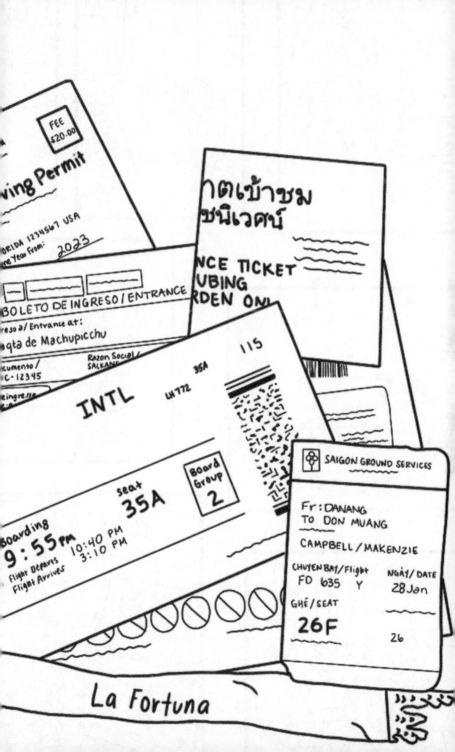

GROWING UP

ON GROWING UP

It's october 19th, 2023, at 12:55 in the morning, and i'm sobbing on my made bed. it's my birthday, and i'm turning twenty-four. which in reality is twenty-four young years but in a nostalgic existential crisis is basically a wrinkling eternity. billie's "getting older" is playing from the speaker in the corner of my room. her words echo off the walls and go straight to my head. "i'm getting older." i'm getting older! i'm getting older and i don't know what to do with myself. i don't know what to make of the last year that's come and gone. time flies so fast it's given me whiplash. i've cried like this for three years in a row now. midnight strikes and the tears are cued. when did birthdays become so somber? how am i supposed to deal with my finiteness? how am i supposed to make sense of it with so little time and so little proof of anything?

it's funny how i've spent most of my life dreaming of growing up when all i do is ache for my girlhood. i long for the days without responsibility, for the days without knowing how cruel the world can be. for the time when everything was new and beautiful and pure. when did i become a woman? where was the sign-up sheet? i don't remember inking my name as trade to become an adult. where i used to have dolls i now have bills. where i used to have recess, i now have hurried lunch breaks before rushing back to my nine-to-five. i'm growing up while feverishly holding on to my childhood. do people know how to let that go? do people know how to hold on to both? to balance them? to let them take turns in the driver's seat?

it's not all bad. but it is all scary. the more i age, the more i grow into a knowledgeable, well-rounded person. the more i can figure out my values and what i believe in, independent of what i was taught growing up— which may or may not be the same things. i have the adult power of making a difference in the areas that mean the most to me. i can become the woman my younger self fantasized about. my childhood dreams are finally coming to the surface. i can touch them and actualize them in ways i couldn't before. when i was a child and the adults would ask me what i wanted to be when i grew up, i would always answer, "a pop star like hannah montana!

or a writer." i'm so incredibly lucky to be one of the people who had their childhood dream come true. six-year-old me, with her first story on her desk in her lopsided handwriting, would be jumping up and down if she could see me now.

but growing up also means coming to know the ache of loss. it means having family members pass away. it means understanding your parents' mortality. i watched someone who lives in a different state from their parents count the number of holidays they might have left to share, and i broke down crying. i know the discomfort that comes with realizing your heroes are human. that your parents and your uncles and your aunts all have flaws. that you, yourself, have flaws too. of learning how to navigate these realizations. i know the gnawing feeling of watching your younger siblings grow up in fragments. of living down the hall from your oldest, closest friend and then suddenly not living in the same neighborhood as them. and i know the way disappointment looks on familiar faces when you turn out to be something other than what they dreamed for you. sometimes growing up means being brave enough to abandon other people's ideas of you in exchange for congruency in yourself.

and growing up also means confronting our most unforgivable friend: time. the more i age, the more acutely aware i am of her. of how intimidating she is. how unstoppable. how ungiving. it's a complicated relationship. on one hand, i understand that her rigidity is what gives life meaning. our numbered days give significance to the way we choose to pass them. they quantify our values, hobbies, joy, dreams. they make the hours we spend with the ones we love precious.

on the other hand, i want to put her in a chokehold and make her stop. to let me have this moment. to let me live just one day without the lingering of existential fear. some days i forget she exists, and these are my most treasured hours. i feel like a child again, and everything glows with promise. other days, she's so persistently in my head i can't stay in the present. i miss out on the now, thinking about my impending end. maybe at twenty-five i'll learn to cope with it. will someone please tell me you learn to cope with it?

this isn't a cohesive essay. but growing up isn't cohesive or linear. my thoughts around growing up aren't cohesive. how do you make sense of yourself getting older? there is so much beauty and so much longing and so much pain in it. this next chapter of poems is an acknowledgment of that. of what it means to age. what it means to watch your girlhood fade. what it means to live as if every day is borrowed.

because it could be.

because it is.

today is my birthday.
i'm trying to figure out where the last twenty-four years
went. i cashed them all out with no spare change.

where did all the women i was before run off to?
i want to invite them to my party.
i want to hold hands with my girlhood.
what i mean is
i'm grasping for my youth before she slips away.

the adults always told me
time moves quicker
the more you grow up
but nothing could prepare me for the whiplash.

yesterday i was barefoot climbing down the ropes of
the waterfall with the first boy i'd ever loved.
today i am twenty-four
and rent is due
and my friends come over to drink wine.

i'll toast to the future,
to what this year will bring
and all the ways i'll grow,
but what about this past?
when do i get a breath?
i'll blow out the candles
and wish this next year goes by slower
but i know i'll blink and it will be october again.

what did you want to be when you grew up?

where did that dream wander off to?

where did that dreamer go?

maybe growing up is
just a continuous untangling:
what do i want
versus
what was i told to want.
i'm obsessed with the idea of living honestly
but there are certain things
my extended circle
doesn't know about me.
"it's probably safer that way."
safer for who?
as i get older i'm starting to realize that
nothing's safer if it costs your peace.
i was spoon-fed the american dream,
wore my promise ring
as a golden ticket to
Happiness.
you get the grades, you get the degree, you get the
husband, you have the kids.
isn't it perfect?
that image has been wavering
and in the moments where the light doesn't shine
the seeds of my individuality are planted.
do i want this?
do i want *this*?
i was born a free spirit
who came to know anxiety
as her invisible best friend
and she held hands with me
throughout my girlhood.
i was me, shrouded,
but now that i've learned to unclasp her grip
i don't have rose-colored vision,

and i think the time has come
that i allow myself to be brave enough
to watch the perceptions they all have fade
and transform, shapeshift, change
into whatever they want to think!
so long as i am unapologetically me.
so long as i scrap the rule book they gave me
and start writing it from scratch.

what does it mean to age?
does talent age with me?
a mishap turned masterpiece?
a gravel road that led to glass steps
at such a young age.

      at such a young age!
did i reach the mountaintop?
does success have a ceiling?
they ask what i'm more afraid of —
succeeding or failing.
at least one knows when to stop.
is my poetry pruning?
at such a young age?

      you did what when you were seventeen?
      you had your first bestseller before you had
      your first kiss?
it's all out of order.
am i out of order
if i can't keep producing?

      when is the next book coming out?
      when is the next book coming out?
i don't even have a title.

      you don't need a title with a name like that
      and at such a young age!
      it was meant to be.
i got lucky.

      you got talent!
i'm so lucky.

      you're so talented!
are the traits the people say about you true if you don't believe them?
are the people who love you all dishonest?

      but the strangers held you close and whispered
      what you meant to them

and all the strangers are liars too!
the masses are off to the races
to persuade me i'm something worth listening to,
i'm someone worth admiring.
i don't know a goddamn thing!
              and god you were just so young!
that's it! i was young!
does it all get better with age?
does it all crumble?
when does it stop?
do i stop?
when will my imposter syndrome get bored of me?
when will it let me live quietly?
when will i be able to see myself not through the lens
of my insecurity?
when is enough enough?
when am i enough
for me?

my sister asked me,

        "don't you ever want a break?"

i told her i took one last week. all sunday i slept in.

        "that's not what i meant."

she meant,

        you just graduated. you have this whole, empty
summer and you've filled it right up to the brim. don't
you ever want a whole season gone of responsibility?

and i told her i don't know how
to not keep my hands busy.
i told her i'm running out of time.
I'M RUNNING OUT OF TIME, don't you see?

i have some odd number of years left to learn
everything and be everything i want to be.
and i don't know how to cope with it.

my sister and i will never share the same wall again.

not for more than a weekend.
not for more than a moment.
i used to roll my eyes when she would
bust through the door and
jump on my bed with her latest great idea.
god what i would give to
have her wreck my room now.
steal all my clothes.
i would trade all the privacy in the world
to know her as intimately as i once did.
we all knew this day was coming.
it's a reality of life.
but to hear about it and to know the ache
as deeply as i now do
are two very different things.
it's a punch to the gut,
it's a gasping for air,
to know that living the life i need to lead
independently is to sacrifice a space
in the closest relationship i will ever know.

it's the balancing act of guilt
and the need to be untethered.
just because you grew up there
doesn't mean you have to stay forever.
soon the suburban lawns and HOAs
start to feel like a trap,
so you move to a big city all alone
to find your own two feet to stand on.
the metallic taste of the skyline
might weather you down.
you'll miss when your sister was across the hall.
she's a missed phone call now.
the busy streets and standstill traffic
just might break your back
but as you fall you'll soon find
the people who'll give you a safe place to land.
they'll open their heart to you,
a friend without conditions.
you'll find your place, you'll claim your space,
you'll live without omissions.
the city feels like home now
and you're lucky to have two,
but remember where you came from
and to still visit the one that built you.

i caught a plane to my dad's homeland. a place he hasn't visited in twenty-four years. the last time he stepped foot here i was just a concept in my mother's belly. my birth was the beginning of a new family to focus on. but the one he has here never forgot about him even when he thought they had. his return was met with the prideful faces of familiar strangers. arms flinging around shoulders and jaws sunk at the man he's become.

i was sitting in the back seat of our borrowed car. we were on our way to denali. i wanted to see the mountains and my dad drove me to chase them down. his father sat in the passenger. i caught my dad laughing. not the polite chuckle you give to appease people. a real, hearty laugh. swapping stories on all the life they've missed. there had been a lot of it. grandpa hadn't always been there and dad hadn't always been forgiving. i'm not sure how my dad felt about this moment. but i can tell you that witnessing that from the back seat felt a lot like a homecoming. and in a lot of ways brought me closer to my father. to see where he'd bruised his knees and learned to ski and scaled the side of his house at seven years old to sneak out with his school friends. to watch him reminisce on his playground. to feel the remnants of his childhood heart in a place he once called home. i can tell you with full confidence that my aunts and uncles were sure happy to have him. and i was happy to discover a family i hadn't known was there. one that is full of love and laughter and a bit of crazy. one that held out their arms to me, a stranger, and my father, and said,

"come here, darling, you're family."

TO HAVE THE FINGERTIPS OF YOUTH
GRAZE YOUR BARE SKIN
TO HAVE THE FACADE OF INVINCIBILITY
CLING ITSELF TO YOU SO FIERCELY YOU
WHOLEHEARTEDLY BELIEVE IN ITS POWER

my knees are curled up to my chest
like they're supposed to rest there,
like they were moments before
the first light touched me,
before i cried for the first time,
my mother holding her breath waiting for that song,
relief when i finally sang it.
now when i sing the song of sorrow
my mother's breath gets caught in her throat.
i'm afraid she'll choke on it
because there is no relief.
i'm acutely aware of my humanity
and my finiteness
and my mother

       who knows how to smooth out my hair and
       hold me and the weight of my grievances,
       who knows how to gently pull them from my
       anxious fingers until they feel small and my
       mother's love feels big.

she doesn't know how to soothe this out of me.
she doesn't know how to help me cope with it.
after all, she is human
and i live six states away now.
my anxious fingers may not know how to
handle my impending death,
but they know how to hang up the phone after
convincing everyone i love i am okay.
they know how to hold my knees tightly while i
convince myself
i am okay,
i am okay,
i'll be okay.

rock myself to the rhythm of my folk song.

i am okay,
i am okay,
i'll be okay.

it's growing pains,
learning to not cast my shadow over her.
to not give advice when it's not needed.
to refrain from becoming her umbrella from the
cruelty of the world.

she tells me, "i can withstand this!"
but i whisper,
                              you don't have to. i'll endure for you.

i used to tell her fables laced with metaphors
as a guide to her girlhood.
now she chronicles nights out in her early twenties
to me like bedtime stories.

she used to come creeping in the night whispering
about her scary dreams. i'd open the covers and feel
her crawl inside my sanctuary half asleep.

we live six states away now.

and everyone talks about the parents.
the empty nest they have to hold.
the image of their little child disappearing.

but no one talks about the ache that comes with being
the eldest and leaving.

watching the littles grow up in fragments.
every returned holiday a piece of a picture
of who they're becoming.

i want the whole picture.

i want the whole damn gallery.

it's a pride and it's a grieving.

since when did you trade
your pink and white light-up skechers
for the clicking high pumps?

since when did you become a woman?

i wonder how long the salamander cave we used to
hunt in has been untouched.

i promise i'll do my grieving in quiet,
let you grow and change and become,
if you promise to not lose our childhood in the
process.
to call me when you think of it.
to ask me, when i return for thanksgiving, to go search
for those lizards again like we did when we were
young.

a new indie folk song finds a shuffle in my playlist
and i break outside to go watch the winged creatures take flight.
an hour passes and i'm still staring at
the tree her little feet flew from forty minutes ago.
i don't know how to draw myself out of this moment,
how to interject myself back into consumer life.
it all moves so fast i forget that there are
beings who know the song in slow motion.
nature is a lullaby i long for,
the wind weaving through my hair,
the trees whispering to each other,
the alto of the river.
and the birds know this and the crickets and the squirrels and the wolves.
i want to be one who knows it.
am i too late? has the world taken it all too far?
i want to live where the quiet things live.
i want more than a moment to be present.

THE THING ABOUT LEAVING IS

it's always there. there's always an end in order and we
know that from the beginning, but from there it all
feels so far away. once you get up close to it, only then
do you realize how ugly and promising and exciting
and gut-wrenching it all is.

goodbyes are a part of life but i'd swear on mine that
not one has been as difficult as this. it's the end of an
era. this is where i lost myself again and again and
rediscovered her. i always found her, in a different light.

this isn't just a goodbye to a place or a person but
goodbye to all the past versions of myself that existed
within these city limits. to each of you, i'm proud.
and so tomorrow we'll throw up our caps
and our professors will say, "those four went by fast,"
as if the number four does it justice.

please know in my head i'm measuring the time i spent
here, not in years, but in the magnitude of olivia's
laugh. in the spontaneity of our youth. in the number
of times brenna swung my bedroom door open with
her convincing smile and dragged me out on a tuesday
night. in the tender moments of tears cried and the
realization that if i had a lifetime with these people, i'd
still be begging for more. more three a.m. talks and madeline
wrapping her hand in mine to run through the
midnight sprinklers across reaney park. more of
sidney's overpoured tequila shots on game day. and
screaming for a sport i only tangentially like because
what else is there to do on a saturday except go where

your friends go because you follow the love they give.
and you'll sit with ashlyn months before and talk
excitedly about where you'll go and how you've grown
but now that it's here it all feels wilted. endings never
come without pain. beginnings never start without
purges.

so i'll keep in touch and promise i'll call
even though we all know my phone feels like a cage.
but i promise i'll try to call,
is that better?
and i'll drive away,
all my bags packed,
see you all waving in the rearview mirror,
and think
if in the next chapter i meet people half as good as the
ones i met here, i think life will turn out pretty okay.

pretty spectacular, even.

GROWING FORWARD

ON GROWING FORWARD

I saved this essay for the very last minute. i wrote the poems, i signed the book deal, i sent over my cover ideas, i even wrote my acknowledgments before i sat down to be here in this moment. it's a tender one. this essay is a mirror held up to all the past versions of me. my gentle reflection. it's a love letter addressed in my name. it's taken a lot for me to get here. to be this honest. to be this brave.

as a child, i lived unafraid. i was curious and clumsy and full of wonder. the world hadn't yet touched me. i was touching the world. anything i could get my sticky little hands on. i spent my days barefoot in the sun, exploring. my cousin and i passed the afternoons digging up roly-polies in the backyard and making little grass homes for them in grandma's old tupperware. when we got bored, we'd run over to our neighbor's to play with any of her fourteen pets. i had no problem knocking. i had no problem talking to strangers without a flutter in my chest. my mom likes to tell the story of when i saw two men dressed in cowboy hats and boots to match at the far end of our local starbucks parking lot. i yelled across to them, "howdy cowboys," in my best four-year-old southern accent and gave them a salute. she was embarrassed. i was next to her, beaming. i was outgoing. i was funny. i was unfiltered. i was so many things back before i knew what it meant to be conscious of me.

as a girl, fear found its way to my fingertips and interlocked our hands. i became aware of other people's perceptions of me. i became afraid of them. i became chained to them. there was this need to be liked by everyone i met. which meant i needed to know the answers to every question my teacher posed in class. i had to know exactly when to dribble and when to pass to my teammates. i needed to learn the language of tween-age girl, the right moment to place a joke, the best time to ask the question. i lived inside my head. i made a home there with just enough room for me and my cavernous anxiety. i became quiet. painfully shy. a shell of the kid i used to be. i had straight As and a small group of friends and soccer games on the weekends, but often it felt like going through the motions. or maybe it didn't then, but looking back now i've colored the memory as complacency. there were so many good moments, but there were also so many moments where i didn't feel like me. where i'd hold my tongue out of fear of rejection or judgment. where i'd do the things i was supposed to do even if i didn't fully believe in them.

i wasn't always kind to myself, and i wasn't always true to myself. or maybe i didn't know how to be, because i didn't yet know who i was.

it took going to university, being forced to think introspectively, my first relationship, first breakup, and first heartbreak to begin to learn who i am. and there were growing pains. i had to outgrow people. i had to outgrow outdated ideas. i had to take a magnifying glass to every aspect of my life: my thoughts, my actions, the friends i'd made, the habits i'd formed, and the whys behind all of them. it was a reconciling. i'd try on different adjectives to see if they fit. swap out new hobbies. one week i'd think i'd got it right and then the next, i would be drowning in what-ifs. i was in a constant state of questioning. my womanhood awakening drastically helped me piece things together, but that was only one part of my identity. and it wasn't all in one swift motion. there were months of stagnancy amid small moments of growth. there were periods i didn't think to look in the mirror. ignorance is a bliss but it's also a dormancy. sometimes it's easier to keep things the way they are, to stay in that comfort. but i've come to know the hard instances as the most exciting. they've always led to growth. they've always led to something greater—even if it's down the road.

it took a long time for me to grow into my skin. to become outgoing again like i was as a little kid. to rediscover my curiosity. i'm less concerned with people's perceptions of me, though i'm still working on abandoning the idea altogether. i'm not sure if i'll ever get there, but i'll keep catching myself in my thinking and i'll keep trying. a year ago, i wouldn't have been able to write this book. there are some people who still think i'm devoutly abstinent and a churchgoing christian. (not that there is anything wrong with those things—they just aren't me.) there's a gnawing in my stomach each time i see them. i've let the fear of hurting them or the idea they hold of me keep me from my full authenticity. but as i continue to grow, i continue to become less afraid. i see the beauty in becoming. the strength in being

as i am, out loud. the power in my own acceptance of it—of me. me! i'm
starting to figure out who i want to be.

if i could, i'd gather all the younger versions of me and collect all their
hands in mine. i'd tell them thank you. i'd tell them i'm sorry. for the years
they stood with me. for the years i was mean. i'd tell them, "look, we made
it! but we're not done becoming." and as i held them, i'd wonder who the
older version of me will be. what she'll look like. when she'll come to visit.
when she'll take my palms in hers with an all-knowing smile and say,

"you'll never believe where we are now!"

THE SPACE I TAKE UP FINALLY FEELS LIKE IT'S
MINE TO CLAIM

headed south
down the PCH.
i drove this way once on my way to you.
this time the freeway is laced with freedom.
i like the way the air tastes down here.
i've thought of migrating,
a fleeting idea,
something we used to talk about,
but now it's for an entirely different reason.
it's comforting to know that i can still make a home
in the places we used to occupy.

i struggle finding my identity in large groups of people.
all i am is wiped away and i adopt the little gestures of
everyone else as if that will make up for my absence. as
if abandoning myself is a belonging.

the way he pronounces his t's in words is mimicked in
my mouth. her hands thrown up as she laughs means
my fingers will follow.

and i'll steal all these mannerisms as if they're my own
to make up for how lost i am between the bodies.

i'm not sure how to stand my ground in a sea of
people.

i'm not sure i have solid enough ground to stand on.

i'm having an identity crisis yet again
and i'm blurring between the lines.
i look in the mirror
and i see myself change shape
at every slight movement,
like a lenticular photo.
i used to love those as a kid.
maybe it was the universe's warning:
> "YOU WILL BECOME WHAT YOU LOVE
> AND YOU WILL HATE IT."

i used to never color in the lines.
my grandma always asked why.
"it's prettier when you do it neatly."
she took my brown crayon and said,
> "like this,"
as she moved across the page.
how i wish i had her steady hand now
to color me straight
because at this very moment
i feel like a kaleidoscope of chaos
in this vast void of being lost
that i can't climb out of.

"tell me about yourself,"
she says.
"who are you?"
she asks
in our interview.
it's only the first question and i've already sunk into
myself.

how do you answer a question you don't have an answer to.

a question you're still asking yourself.

"i am everything and nothing and all that's in between.
i am quiet and outgoing,
adventurous but not too risky.
i'm resolute but i never know what i want."

some days all my adjectives lie in a bed and undress
and make love so ferociously i don't know which is
which.

(and if you ask me again tomorrow
my answer will be different.)

i'm dancing on the edge of throwing it all away

i met picasso.

he came to me in my dream last night.

he took my hand in his and said,

>"sweet girl, i must paint you."
>"sweet girl, you are the most perfect subject."
>"sweet girl, you are the most wonderful
>evidence of abstract."

"i look at you and i see blue jays singing upon your
shoulder. i watch flowers trade the sun for your smile.
how infectious your joy is.

and i look at you and i see crows digging their claws
into your collarbone as they chant into your ear. i see a
forecast of rainfall for the next seven days. i see the
plants in your garden wilting.

i see tyrants of wars bowing at your feet.
and, yet, i see how viciously you beg on your knees
for an old love to stay.

i see the way goosebumps form when you are amongst
art. the way your eyes glimmer just looking at it.
and i see you recoil at the art in your mirror.

sweet girl, i look at you and i see shipwrecks and peace
offerings and gunshots fired.

i see you wave your white flag and see the shadow of
your beckoning fighter.

i see a landscape of greenery and forest fires.

with you, everything is
                                                    and isn't.

with you, everything is a paradox.

and oh, sweet girl, what a lovely portrait you would
make."

"it all means nothing
if you have no one to share it with"
is true in theory.

but can't i share it with myself?

aren't i enough?

no one told me
how hard it was gonna be
to find myself

because it's not a quick fix or a onetime thing.
it's finding and refinding and redefining and every time
you think you've got it
it's all wrong.
or it's half right laced with white lies you believe in,
and i'm searching for an end that doesn't exist,
a finish line that's only marked by death,
the thought of which
sends me into an existential crisis
and i'm trying to learn to get comfortable
in things less linear.
can someone tell me if it gets easier after twenty-two?
i know we're all making it up as we go
but it'd be kind if you'd lie and say
i'll know Everything on my thirtieth birthday,
a marker to look forward to,
something to make growing older feel less like
an emptying hourglass.
seven and a half years until then
to search for everything i think i am
and everything i'm not
and the in-betweens,
and yet i know when i get there
i'll have to start all over again
while time continues slipping.

today i feel that every version of myself

is singing in unison

and oh what a beautiful choir they make

i'm trying my best to describe the feeling but it's
bubbling and changing shape at every sleight of hand.
and it's confusing to be everything at once.
it's also the most free i've felt in the entirety of my
existence.
i'm working on not compartmentalizing.
i used to think putting everything in a box
was a saving grace
but now i only know it as safe
and i know safe as suffocating.

the moment i started blurring the lines was the
moment i was reborn,
and how bright and beautiful and eclectic is the act of
being alive, unapologetically.

dear mama,

i'm falling in love again.

and before you roll your eyes i need you to listen when
i say this time is different.

i'm finding beauty in all her crevices and flaws. the
curves of her body are artwork. her smile a delicate
song. all the things she hates about herself i'm learning
to love. her stubbornness translated into passion. her
quiet into observation. her idealism into someone who
relentlessly reaches out to the world for more.

i'm falling in love with myself.

and oh what a beautiful thing to find light within me
instead of searching for it in someone else.

i know you're probably sick of reading letters to a past version of me. how many words could i write? when will they run out? i'd tell you i'm tired of writing them but it'd be a lie. there's something tender about gifting the younger version of you grace. she needed so much love.

i'm in the dubai airport right now. i'm about to fly back to the states. but not before i dramatically look out the window at the sunrise and allow myself the space to hold this moment.

> why do you think i write? i'm feverishly trying
> to hold everything together.

i spent the past few days speaking to a younger generation about poetry. about my story. about what it all means to me. about how scared i was to be seen.

i saw myself in the reflection of their questions. i saw myself in the reflection of their skin. sitting at their desks, writing with the distant dream to give this little life meaning. they have so many aspirations. they are so young, intelligent, capable.

i was too.
and i was so mean. quick to inflict insult. rub salt in my own wounds. criticize every conversation, critique every mistake. i wish i could take her hands and show her now how bright everything turned out to be. how lovely it all is on the other side. she never would have guessed we'd make it here — and yet.

she didn't know better then. but i know better now. and it's in these moments that i try to hold her and heal the parts of her that were hurting.

she is so beautiful
and in my mind
she's somewhere smiling.

a (final) letter to the past versions of me:

did you think you'd make it here? what once was a distant dream is now graspable. beyond graspable. you've got it. you've made it. you made it happen. i'm so fucking proud of you. i wish i would have told you that sooner. i'm sorry for all the years i was mean.

this is a new phase. one where you're honest and open and trying really, really hard to find the balance between acceptance and growth. i pray it sticks.

i used to want to be rid of you. some of you, at least. if i could have drunk a magic potion to make you disappear, i would have.

i'm glad there was no magic potion.

because i'm learning that i needed each and every one of you at that time. there was no alternative. you were as you were, i was as i was, and that's how it needed to be. without you, i would not be who i am today. each of you learned lessons i needed to learn and responded in ways i needed to respond. even if looking back it was wrong, in that moment, you were human.

i don't think i'll ever shed any of you. not entirely. nor would i want to. we are all interlocked and layered in too many intricate ways. you are me and i am you and we are us, and i'm proud to hold each one of you under my skin.

so here's to us. to all of you and all we've been through and all the times you've carried me onwards. for all the ways you've shaped and reshaped me into the woman i am today. each time more humble, more soft, more open. we have more work to do, but so far, i think you've done a fine job.

this is the most me i've ever been
and god does she glimmer

FINAL NOTE FROM THE AUTHOR

(you know, in case you haven't gotten enough of me),

i promise you're nearly done with the book. i just have one more thing. i want to give space to my gratitude. thank you for holding the intimate parts of me. thank you for giving me a place to lay it out.

for those of you that have read previous work of mine, thank you for still being here. thank you for making me feel like i belong. thank you for giving my work meaning. you make my little writing dream a reality and i deeply appreciate you more than you will ever know. and i love you!

for those of you that are new readers, welcome! you now have a very up-close and personal glimpse into my life. how beautiful that two singular humans get to share that? thank you for choosing to be here. and i love you, too!

this collection has been incredibly cathartic for me. it's been a journey. a hell of a long time coming. i'm so proud of what i've built and where i've come. and i'm so proud of wherever you are in your coming-of-age story. however it's unfolding, i know it's leading you where you're meant to be. i can't wait to see where it takes you. i can't wait to see what you make of it. i may never know you the way you now know me, but i know there are similarities between us. and for me, that's enough to be rooting for you.

until next time.

THE GRATITUDE CORNER

this book would not be possible without michelle halket, beau adler, jessica peirce, molly ringle, and the rest of the central avenue team. thank you for having relentless support and faith in me. working with you has always been such a pleasure. you make my little ideas become big, tangible things!

thank you to all my friends (madison, macie, jordan, emma, virginia, cat, so many of you!) who read and reread different essays and poems while i anxiously texted you every few days asking if you liked it. you all lift me up so much and my love for you is SO BIG.

to my parents—thank you for allowing me the space to grow. thank you for supporting me even when it can be uncomfortable. thank you for growing with me and giving me light with your unconditional love.

to the rest of my family and friends who very well may have learned some new things about me—i love you and i hope this only gave you more space to better understand me in ways that i fail to verbally communicate. oh, and did i mention i love you? <3

Makenzie Campbell is an author from Seattle, who has been writing since she first learned the alphabet. At eighteen, in the chaos of her high school senior year, she released her first collection, *2am Thoughts*, which was a massive success. This was followed by *Nineteen* and *Rooms of the Mind*. Now in Denver, she's learning to navigate the labyrinth of her twenties. When she's not writing or having an existential crisis, she can be found exploring the mountains, pursuing a master's in mental health, or packing her 21-liter backpack to explore new lands.

@makenzie.campbell.poetry